PORTRAIT OF AN OWL

My tales of Mat

Edited by
Ann Snook and Richard Wilson

Gresham

First Published in 2012 by Gresham Publications
in association with
The Friends of Christchurch Park, Ipswich

www.focp.org.uk

*A catalogue record of this book is available from the
British Library*

Snook, Reg
Portrait of an Owl/Reg Snook

Printed by Tuddenham Press Ltd.

ISBN 978-0-9561080-2-9

Sweet Suffolk owl, so trimly dight
With feathers like a lady bright;
Thou sing'st alone, sitting by night,
Te whit! Te whoo!

Thy note that forth so freely rolls
With shrill command the mouse controls,
And sings a dirge for dying souls:
Te whit! Te whoo!

Thomas Vautor (*fl.*1592-1619)

Contents

Introduction 1

Mabel 3

Why does Mabel disappear each year? 5

What does Mabel eat? 8

"There was an old owl liv'd in an oak" 11

My introduction to owls 17

The Wildlife Inspectorate 21

Tawny Owl 25

Common Barn Owl 31

Little Owl 37

Short-Eared Owl 41

Long-Eared Owl 45

Mrs Goudy and the Hawk Owl 49

Eagle Owl 53

Snowy Owl 57

Where to see owls in Suffolk 60

Epilogue 63

Owl terminology 68

Wildlife index 71

About the author 72

ACKNOWLEDGEMENTS

My particular thanks go to Ann Snook for her unstinting support and encouragement, and to Richard Wilson for his additional research and expertise in preparing the text for publication. Thanks also to Paul Sherman, not only for his wonderful photographs of Mabel but also for his diligence in locating her family. Special thanks go to Mrs Rene Goudy, who provided me with the most unique and perhaps bizarre birdwatching experience of my life.

Portrait of an Owl is dedicated to Mabel: without her this book would never have been written.

INTRODUCTION

Owls have always held a fascination for me. Inspired by Mabel, the tawny owl who has captured the hearts of all who have seen her in Ipswich's Christchurch Park, I decided to write about my life with these magical and intriguing hunters.

I was about eight years old and a member of a local 'gang' when I was encouraged by my mates to climb through a hedge to investigate a large hole in an old oak tree. The oak in question stood where the Suffolk Show is now held every year, at Trinity Park on the Bucklesham Road near Ipswich. Being rather adept at climbing, I was usually the one chosen to shin up a tree (though I always found coming down a much more difficult part of the operation). Anyway, the climb up to that particular hole is still very clear in my mind. The commotion I made was clearly too much for a tawny owl incubating her eggs in the tree and, with a whoosh, the bird fled, its face and mine only inches apart. I managed to cling to the edge of the hole and, peering inside, found four glossy white tawny owl eggs and a dead rat. It goes without saying that at the sight of a large brown bird fleeing the oak tree the rest of my gang ran off along the hedgerow, leaving me to descend without help (as usual...). Nevertheless, that experience has stayed with me all my life.

This was the first tawny owl's nest that we found in that spring of 1946, and it was not the only time we discovered food along with the eggs and young. One nest we found at Martlesham Creek on the River Deben held three eggs and a fish! I can't remember the species of fish but the owl had probably found it dead at the water's edge. I don't imagine that a tawny owl is capable of 'doing an osprey', that is, plunging into the water to grab a live fish. Not all the openings we came upon were homes to birds: one suitable looking hole I found contained a hornets' nest, something I discovered only after I had climbed far up into the tree. My friends departed the scene in even more of a hurry than usual, convinced (as we all were at that tender age) that if you were stung twice by a hornet, then you'd die! Again I descended on my own – though this time at some speed. Amazingly I was not stung even once as, thankfully, the hornets took no notice of me.

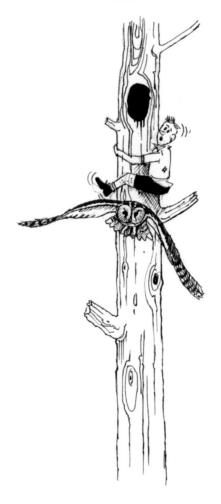

MABEL

Mabel, Ipswich's famous tawny owl, was first 'discovered' in Christchurch Park at about 8am on Monday, 22 September 2008 by Richard Stewart, a keen naturalist and butterfly expert. She was sitting in a very visible spot, in an appropriately sized hole some ten metres up an old oak tree. Thereafter, our friendly owl was seen more and more often, so much so that it was suggested that she deserved a name. Schoolchildren were invited to make suggestions and a three-year-old young lady named Anouk came up with the name of 'Mabel'. For this she was rewarded with a Winnie-the-Pooh hot water bottle! This was in 2009 and since then Mabel has been a star. She has been photographed many thousands of times, appearing in national newspapers and magazines.

Well, I say 'she'… Because the owl was so named by our young friend, it was always assumed that Mabel was female. In fact it is quite difficult to distinguish between a male and a female tawny owl from a distance. When viewed close together, the female often appears slightly larger than the male, although this is not necessarily the case. Since Mabel was always seen on her own it was difficult at first to state categorically that Mabel was female. However this now seems almost certain as, in successive years, young tawny owls have been found very close to Mabel's roost, reinforcing the view that she is one of a pair that regularly breeds here. In fact, one such youngster was found at the foot of the very oak tree where the roost hole is located. Luckily for the young tawny owl in question, it was gingerly carried to Park Manager, Sam Pollard, who wisely sent it to the Suffolk Owl Sanctuary at Stonham Barns for a check-up. Nothing appeared to be wrong with the owlet and so it was returned to the Park and, with the help of a long ladder, it was placed back in the oak tree but this time high up as Sam feared that a dog could quite easily savage it. After being put out of harm's way, the owlet promptly flew off! Although young tawny owls appear to be just a ball of fluff when they are a few weeks old, they are in fact quite capable of climbing trees using their talons and beak. The flight feathers (primaries and secondaries) grow very rapidly which means that, as was the case with this particular tawny owlet, they can fly short distances even at a young age.

WHY DOES MABEL DISAPPEAR EACH YEAR?

Every year, around the beginning of spring, Mabel disappears for some weeks. At first we thought that she might have perished or moved elsewhere but, for the last four years, she has reappeared again in late spring much to the delight of Park visitors. We now believe that she is indeed a female and that she starts to incubate her eggs at that time of year. Until recently, it has always seemed to be the same owl perching atop the old oak tree. However, during the weekend of 24 February 2012, 'Mabel' in the roost was certainly not the Mabel we knew – the bird did not have her markings or colouration. Yet by the following week 'our' Mabel was definitely back in position. If we assume that Mabel is one of a pair and that she breeds in that particular oak tree near to Westerfield Road, then it is quite possible that, from time to time, Mabel's mate visits the nest hole and so is sometimes on view. Maybe her companion is much shyer and does not seek to be nationally famous!

Paul Sherman, who has photographed Mabel on numerous occasions, has heard an owl in Mabel's tree 'hooting'. We know that male tawny owls hoot, but not females. By this I mean that the male tawny owl is the one that gives the long drawn out 'hooo' call. The female replies with 'ke-wick'. Nearly four hundred years ago, the Elizabethan composer Thomas Vautor described the call as 'Te whit! Te whoo!' which is how most people might describe a tawny owl's call today. However, it could be that Vautor in so describing the tawny owl's call was combining those of both the male and the female. In the past, when I kept numerous disabled wild tawny owls, I recorded a wide range of call notes. I observed that a female tawny owl would utter a long, low quavering call that could be interpreted as a 'soft hoot'.

To make matters even more confusing, three reports were given to me of two adult tawny owls being seen together in the roost hole – perhaps Mabel and her mate? Judging by the tawny owl calls that can be heard at certain times of the year, I would suggest that Mabel and her partner are just one of several pairs of tawny owls in the vicinity of Christchurch Park. Two years ago the body of a tawny owl was brought into the Reg Driver Visitor Centre in the Park which had sadly died after flying into a window of a house less than a mile from Mabel's roost. At the time, Mabel had done one of her disappearing acts and I rather foolishly told the staff at the Centre that the dead owl could be the Park's favourite bird. Two days later, Mabel miraculously reappeared...

So we assume that Mabel is a female, she has a mate (tawny owls are monogamous) and they produce young each year. In captivity, tawny owls can live for up to twenty years but in the wild this is much less likely because of all the dangers they face. We can also assume that Mabel disappears deeper into the hole in the tree below her roost in the spring to raise chicks. Of course, up until 2012 these were only assumptions because tawny owls are known to change their roosting sites. We now know that these assumptions were correct: Mabel was simply busy rearing a family.

We are so used to seeing Mabel just sitting in her tree that we tend to forget that she is a flying (and killing) machine. Every autumn we have a huge firework display in the Park organised by the local scouts. On one occasion a couple of years ago, Park Manager Sam Pollard was standing beneath Mabel's roost where, to all intents and purposes, she appeared asleep. According to Sam, as soon as the first firework exploded, Mabel was off, flying speedily across the Westerfield Road and away.

"As soon as the first firework exploded,
Mabel was off..."

WHAT DOES MABEL EAT?

Tawny owls will only breed if there is enough food available. Despite Mabel using her well-known roost for over three years, until the spring of 2012 I had no evidence to help me determine her diet. I should have found pellets, which are the roughage and indigestible bones that an owl regurgitates after swallowing its food whole. A tawny owl will usually produce two such pellets over a twenty four hour period. Yet, although Mabel sits in such a position that a regurgitated pellet ought to fall down to the grass below, I found not even one. Does Mabel cough up her pellets inside the hollow tree? She would have to turn around to do so which is extremely unlikely. Could it be that something or someone removes the pellets? Maybe the early morning dog walkers have the answer? Are the pellets eaten by their dogs or foxes or even by our numerous grey squirrels? None of these seemed a likely explanation but nevertheless it was very unusual not to find any pellets.

The importance of finding pellets is that these would tell us what Mabel eats. For a long time we could only surmise that her diet consisted mainly of rodents as we know that rats are common in the Park and in the nearby gardens. However, a tawny owl diet would usually contain only about twenty per cent rats. So what else does she and the other town owls eat? What about mice? Yes, there are house mice available in nearby gardens, and in mine there are wood mice. I have also been brought a yellow-necked mouse from this area. So Mabel could be eating both mice and rats. I have no record of shrews in this vicinity but doubtless there are some.

If Mabel were to hunt over the Park as well as the nearby gardens she could supplement her diet with roosting songbirds. Of course, I put the blame for the disappearance of the Park's ducklings fairly and squarely on the shoulders of the notorious lesser black-backed and herring gulls. But I am sure that Mabel would willingly grab with both talons the opportunity to snatch one or more mallard ducklings. (Owls use their talons to transport larger animals whilst smaller prey is carried off in the bill.) She would also take moles which regularly turn up in neighbouring gardens.

I doubt if she would tackle a grey squirrel, although she might have a go at a baby. There are rabbits in one area of the Park (although their numbers are declining rapidly due to the rising number of urban foxes), so young rabbits might well be on the menu. Our tawny owls might also catch and devour earthworms. The Park and the surrounding gardens might easily support various families of tawnies but, frustratingly, until I found pellets, then I would have no proof of what they were eating.

Then in May of 2012 some of our questions were answered when at last we found some pellets. These consisted of a great deal of fur and many small, assorted bones. Three jawbones were discovered in the pellets and, on close examination, these were found to be from a house mouse, a wood mouse and a young rat. Alongside the pellets were approximately thirteen centimetres of undigested intestine from an adult rat. Two weeks later, more pellets were found consisting almost entirely of the remains of adult rats. After four years of speculation, at last we could begin to answer the question of what Mabel eats.

But what about drink? Owls only rarely drink as they get most of the moisture they need from their prey. Tawnies are the only British owls that regularly bathe, in puddles, ponds or even water butts. Some will come to grief by drowning when their feathers become waterlogged and they are unable to climb free of the water so it is unlikely that Mabel would attempt to bathe in Christchurch Park's steeply edged Round Pond. But she might use the shallow areas of smaller ponds in nearby gardens or possibly even the Wilderness Pond.

Threat display of a tawny owl
incubating eggs

"THERE WAS AN OLD OWL LIVED IN AN OAK..."

In the past I have expressed my surprise that Mabel has survived so long. By that I mean that a tawny owl's life can be quite perilous. In my youth I found tawny owls strung up with other species of owls on gamekeepers' gibbets. Tawny owls will take young pheasants, especially if the pheasant chicks are in an open enclosure near to a wood. Because of this, even today, tawny owls are illegally caught in pole traps, a barbaric form of capture. Of course tawnies are more likely to be found dead in the road. They tend to alight on the roads to scavenge for small animals and birds and then become road casualties themselves. Tawny owls are also in danger of poisoning due to eating contaminated rats and mice. I have even retrieved owls stuck in chimneys and found them caught up in garden netting. Tawnies like to bathe and in so doing they sometimes get waterlogged and drown. We have already seen how owls, like other birds, can perish flying into our glass windows. Mabel has done well to avoid all of these dangers.

And Mabel has successfully bred young. I made an exciting discovery in the spring of 2012. Whilst walking through the Park on 6 May after admiring the annual vintage vehicle rally run by the Ipswich Transport Museum, there was Mabel sitting in her normal roost keenly observing all that was going on. For once she was not asleep. The reason for her state of alertness soon became clear for, perched on one of the lower branches of her oak tree, was a young tawny owl, all fluffy and 'cute'. The youngster was taking not one bit of notice of the many people gathering below her. This was proof positive that tawny owls have bred in the Park and that Mabel disappeared each year to raise young. This youngster was about five weeks old which means that the eggs were probably laid in the latter days of February – quite early for tawnies who will lay four eggs if there is sufficient food available. Perhaps only one young tawny owl had been produced following a particularly dry winter. The next morning the young owlet had gone. The primary and secondary feathers are the first to grow on a baby owl and therefore Mabel's youngster would be quite capable of flying from one tree to another. It was also obvious that Mabel was not inside the hole because stock doves were actually disappearing down it, so it seemed that the young tawny owl had moved away from the roost and Mabel had gone with it.

Around that time several people commented that the owl they saw sitting in the roost appeared quite different to Mabel in both looks and behaviour. Some suggested that it was another owl altogether. However, Paul Sherman who had regularly been photographing our owl produced a photo of Mabel taken on 5 May, just the day before the youngster appeared. I compared it with a photograph taken by Paul in 2011 and the two were more or less identical. Her change in appearance on those occasions might have been because she was agitated at having newly fledged young nearby.

A week later, Paul, finding Mabel's roost hole vacant, was trying to locate her when, in the nearby small trees across the footpath, he found not only Mabel and her youngster but also her mate. The trees in which the owls were perching were quite small therefore giving Paul good views of all three tawnies. This was the first time that a pair of tawnies, plus a youngster, had been seen together: another red-letter day in the story of the owls of Christchurch Park.

The next day was even more exciting – in the same small trees opposite Mabel's roost Paul discovered a total of five tawny owls, two adults and three fluffy youngsters. It was under these trees that we first found some owl pellets. Now we knew for certain that there is enough food in and around our eighty-two acre Park for a pair of tawnies to produce a full clutch of youngsters.

Mabel returned to her roost in the old oak tree in the second week of August 2012, the caring of her offspring obviously over for another season. Many people who gathered under her famous roost remarked on her changed appearance; she looked lighter, fluffier and quite different to the last time she was seen. Some even queried whether or not it was Mabel.

Yes, it was Mabel and this time her changed appearance can be easily explained. Female tawny owls do the incubating and so the male will have had to bring all the food to her while she was sitting on the eggs and when the young were very small. Mabel had been enclosed in that hole in the tree with her youngsters for some weeks. She would have received numerous dead rodents from her mate and torn them up to feed the owlets: a very messy occupation. Even when the young were on the wing, she still had to hunt for prey and offer it to her growing family. She would therefore have become somewhat dishevelled and her feathers very worn. Each year all birds moult out their old feathers and grow new ones. The Mabel that reappeared in August 2012 looked different as she was moulting out her 'old clothes' and her new feathers were coming through.

So the spring of 2012 saw several more parts of the Mabel jigsaw completed. In previous years, we had only seen one owlet in the spring and assumed that if indeed Mabel was the parent she only produced one youngster per year. We never fully appreciated that when young owls leave the nest hole (after about six weeks) they disperse quickly but still remain in their parents' care. We never thought to look up into the branches of the small trees across the way from Mabel's oak.

We also now knew that the adult owls in our Park not only find enough food for themselves but also for rapidly growing families, with both parents hunting for food as the owlets grow bigger. Mabel has been seen for four years now and if she has produced more than one youngster per year, as seems likely, then perhaps over a dozen tawny owls have been forced to find territories in the vicinity of the Park.

All birds have an area of habitat in which they both breed and hunt and most birds will defend this territory vigorously. Young tawny owls will take over territories vacated by other owls, but if suitable areas cannot be found then those tawny owls will not breed and without a steady source of food they will perish. If there are no free territories close to their place of birth then they will have to travel further afield. Of course, many nearby gardens are large enough to hold a tawny owl or two but Mabel and her offspring could also have produced owls for other areas of Ipswich such as the Valley Road, Constitution Hill, the Dales and Broomhill. Judging by the late autumn calls at night, I suspect that there are many more tawny owls in Christchurch Park than just one pair.

If you would like to see some of Paul Sherman's magnificent photographs of Mabel and her offspring, visit the website of the Friends of Christchurch Park: www.focp.org.uk.

Mabel, her partner and their three offspring sitting together in Christchurch Park

*Mabel gazes quizzically down at the Town's
annual Santa run*

MY INTRODUCTION TO OWLS

Fifty years ago I was asked to care for a tawny owl that had been hit by a car. I was able to patch up that road accident victim and it was later released back into the wild. That owl was to be the first of many and soon I became known as an expert on rehabilitating disabled owls and other birds. This I was not! However, by keeping owls in captivity one obviously gathered much knowledge along the way, and I found out many things about owls that you would not find in the average bird book. I learned not only about the birds themselves but also about how to keep disabled birds alive and, perhaps more importantly, how to look after them. Over the subsequent years I cared for many species of owls and birds of prey brought to me chiefly by the RSPB and RSPCA. At first I received just British owls, mainly road casualties, but later I looked after more exotic species that were usually escapees from collections of birds of prey. There was a period of time when I had several species of owl in my care, the total running into several dozen. But it is one thing helping an owl to overcome its disabilities, it is quite another to rehabilitate that bird back into the environment.

Sadly, not all of the birds brought to me could be returned to the wild. An owl has to be in top condition to survive because it must hunt for its food. Yes, owls do scavenge, but a damaged owl that is incapable of hunting will die, so in those early years I accumulated quite a collection of disabled wild owls. It was good for me to be able to study them at close quarters, and I have to admit that in those early years I learned a great deal about birds of prey and especially about British owls, but a permanently damaged owl cannot be released into the wild, where it should be. Over time, my feelings about keeping disabled birds in captivity began to change. Why keep an injured owl when there is no chance of releasing it back into the wild? What sort of life is it for such a majestic bird to be cooped up in an enclosure with no chance of release? As a Wildlife Inspector, I visited keepers of birds of prey who claimed to put the welfare of their birds first but who had in their collection owls and other raptors with severe injuries such as a missing wing, or a badly damaged or deformed leg. The keepers said that they were going to breed from them and of course release the offspring into the wild. I really don't think so!

Apart from the fact that a bird in this condition looks pitiful, keeping it in this state is pointless. Often the reason given for doing so is that the wild disabled bird can be encouraged to breed and the young released. But if the species in question is neither rare nor endangered, what is the point of this, especially if by our actions we consign ill-equipped birds to stressful and short lives in the wild? I gradually realised that there was no proof that a disabled bird patched up and set free or even, for that matter, youngsters bred in captivity, ever survived for long in the wild.

As the years passed I became convinced that the kindest thing to do with a severely disabled owl or kestrel that was brought to me to be 'patched up' would be to put the bird down. As soon as the bird arrived, often brought to me by Inspector Ron Summers of the RSPCA, I would carefully assess its injuries. If it could be rehabilitated then it would receive all the care I could offer, but if that bird could never resume its life in the wild, then it would be dispatched. Does that sound cruel? I think not, especially after seeing so many magnificent birds of prey with parts of limbs missing looking so very doleful in cages.

It was seeing a short-eared owl on a perch in an aviary (that was really a converted chicken run) with a badly broken wing hanging down that changed my view on keeping injured owls in captivity. A short-eared owl in a cage – it was so upsetting. A beautiful bird such as this should be flying free and not sitting pathetically behind wire.

One of the major difficulties when caring for disabled wild birds is that they must be kept well fed. Looking after one or two is not really a problem as it is relatively easy to trap mice and there is always the possibility of finding road kills. However, when you are caring for several owls, with the chance that more might arrive any day, then there is a serious food problem. In my early days I was greatly assisted by a nearby farmer who supplied chickens to supermarkets. The chicks arrived at his farm as day-olds – thousands of them – and over the course of the first few days the mortality rate would be quite high. I was therefore able to freeze large quantities of young chicks for later feeding to my birds. However, chickens intended for the supermarket grow rapidly and their mortality slows down greatly as they do so: my access to food was limited to those first few days.

I know of keepers today who still feed their birds on day-old chicks supplemented with rats and mice but I needed to collect road kills to supplement chicks from the farm. Very sadly it is amazing the amount of wildlife killed on our roads and so my owls were regularly fed on stoats, weasels, moles, rats and even hedgehogs, all of which I had to skin and chop up. An owl which has been injured as a result of an accident is usually suffering from shock and so when a bird first arrived it would have to be force-fed by holding the owl's beak open and pushing small pieces of chopped meat down its throat. After a couple of such sessions, the owl (if it was going to recover) would begin to feed itself. The owls tucked into a varied diet of dead birds, which once, rather surprisingly, included a green budgerigar that had fallen victim to someone's four wheels.

In my younger days I kept wild disabled owls in my artist's studio. There was, however, a downside to this. Back then the studio was in a very large room in what was formerly the barrack block on the disused and as yet undeveloped Martlesham Heath airfield. One New Year's Day I became very unwell. My lungs seemed as though they were on fire and I had great difficulty in either breathing or walking. My doctor diagnosed me as having pneumonia and fortunately, after a course of antibiotics, I recovered. When my doctor later realised that I had been in close contact with owls, he suggested that the cause of the pneumonia was psittacosis, a severe infectious disease characterised by high fever and pulmonary involvement. This is a disease primarily of parrots but it can also affect other species of birds, including owls, and is easily transmissible to man. The lesson I learnt was not to keep owls in my studio!

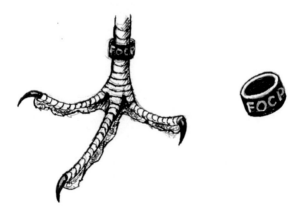

A falcon's foot and leg fitted with a closed ring

THE WILDLIFE INSPECTORATE

I became a Wildlife Inspector for DEFRA (Department for Environment, Food and Rural Affairs) when the Inspectorate was formed in 1982. In recent years this has been wound down somewhat due to the adverse financial climate but, for thirty years, I did my bit to help to protect our most endangered birds of prey. I worked alongside fellow Inspectors such as Bob Scott, Roy Dennis MBE, Paul Llewellyn, Jemima Parry-Jones MBE and Nick Williams, all highly respected in the field of birds of prey conservation.

Falconry is one of the most ancient of pastimes. Let me make this clear: in this country, keeping birds of prey in captivity is completely legal – whatever the moral arguments for or against – as long as those birds have been bred in captivity and the keeper is registered with DEFRA. It was the Inspector's job to check that what the keepers were doing was legal, and in the breeding season we delivered closed rings to the keepers and witnessed the ringing of their birds. A closed ring is a continuous band of bronze coloured metal embossed in white with a unique identifying number that is attached to UK captive chicks before they are ten days old. After that date the hind claw of the bird clicks into place preventing the ring from being placed on the bird's leg. In this country a bird of prey cannot be sold unless it is wearing a closed ring, and if an Inspector finds a bird of prey in the keeper's care that is not wearing a closed ring then it is assumed that the bird has been taken from the wild. Occasionally a ring can cause a bird discomfort and for the bird's safety it has to be cut away. The Inspector then witnesses the replacement ring being put on the bird's leg, but this will not be a closed ring. The embossed number on all DEFRA's rings enables Inspectors to easily identify the birds throughout their lives. It is amazing for me to think that over the years I witnessed the ringing of many hundreds of peregrines, eagles, merlins and goshawks.

I am describing my period of time as an Inspector because it gave me close contact with birds of prey including sundry species of owl both native and non-native. In 1998 the captive barn owl population alone in the UK was thought to be about thirty thousand (whereas in America and Australia it is generally illegal to own a native owl). Many of the keepers I visited kept owls in their aviaries legally and although it was not in my remit to inspect owls (as they are not Schedule IV category birds) I nonetheless had a unique opportunity to observe and learn more about them.

I suppose there will always be criminals in all walks of life but, when the Wildlife Inspectorate was first formed, many unscrupulous keepers were taking the eggs and young of rare birds of prey from the wild including peregrine falcon, golden eagle, goshawk and merlin for large monetary gain. The Inspectorate had immediate success and over the years most of this wildlife crime has been eradicated. The introduction of DNA testing, microchipping and severe penalties for taking birds of prey from the wild were the main factors in the reduction of these crimes, thanks mainly to a dedicated and very knowledgeable band of Inspectors. The introduction of DNA testing was especially effective: if blood taken from a young bird of prey did not match the blood from the alleged parents then that youngster was definitively not the produce of the 'parent' birds and was most probably taken from the wild.

Because of the use of certain noxious chemicals, numbers of peregrines and other birds of prey crashed alarmingly in the 1960's. When the Inspectorate was formed in 1982, birds of prey numbers were still very low. Now, all of our species apart from merlin and hen harrier are on the increase and the Government's Wildlife Inspectorate is one reason for this recovery. There still remain those willing to plunder our magnificent wildlife (and as recently as October 2012 the RSPB named East Anglia one of the worst areas for the persecution of birds of prey) but their numbers have reduced. The Inspectorate was put in place not just to eliminate illegal keepers but also to support the more genuine falconers. I like to think that I can call those keepers that I visited 'my friends'. I certainly learned a huge amount from them and can vouch for the fact that many falconers are top birders and know much more about birds of prey than I ever will.

A peregrine on a falconer's gloved hand

An adult tawny owl

TAWNY OWL

Everyone knows the call of the tawny owl (*Strix aluco*), but the 'hoo-hoo-hoooo' is only that of the male. It is easily reproduced by humans either by a low whistle or, as I did when I was young, by stretching a blade of long, flat grass between the thumb and forefinger of both hands and blowing gently through the gap produced by the thumbs. Come to think of it, having kept tawny owls in my studio, the sounds produced by both of these methods is really nothing like the actual tawny owls' call notes. Heard from close quarters, the male tawny owl's call is much coarser but also much more rounded. The female's call note can be roughly translated as 'ke-wick'.

Mabel is of course a tawny owl, and to her many fans a description of a tawny owl won't be necessary. But I wonder how many of her admirers know that tawnies are dimorphic – that is there are two colour phases, grey and brown. They are quite large birds being about thirty six centimetres in length and, whereas many bird books suggest that both sexes are the same size, I have found that tawny owls vary greatly with the female usually being slightly larger than the male.

Mabel is greatly loved by Park goers and it is not unusual to hear someone passing the time of day with her. I have often wondered what would be the reaction if the person standing under her tree received a reply! Why an owl should be more loved than, say, a mute swan or a mandarin duck, can be simply explained I think. Owls have eyes on the front of their heads (more on owl vision shortly) and they almost look human. But their cuddly appearance hides the fact that owls, including Mabel, are killers. Mabel kills to survive. That fluffy ball of feathers snoozing in the early morning sunlight in that hollow tree becomes at night a very efficient killing machine. She has extremely sharp talons and a powerful beak, with hearing far superior to ours and she flies on silent wings. Her method of catching food is to find a suitable perch and await her prey.

All owls have large eyes (those of a snowy owl weighing about as much as our own) to the front of the head which gives them good stereoscopic vision. In nocturnal species the pupil can be closed to a pinprick in bright light or opened so wide in darkness that the iris virtually disappears. The extraordinary ability of owls to gather light is enhanced in many species by a reflective layer behind the retina called the tapetum lucidum which 'catches' any light that may have been missed. Tawny owls are thought to have the best vision of all owls, indeed of all vertebrates, seeing about a hundred times better than humans in low light. Because of the size and shape of owls' eyes, they cannot move them in their sockets but instead turn their necks some two hundred and seventy degrees horizontally in either direction on surprisingly long and flexible necks.

Tawny owls nest from March onwards, although I have known eggs to be laid as early as December. A hole in a tree is a common nesting site and two to four round white eggs are laid. Normally an egg is laid every two or three days but this can vary, and incubation starts with the laying of the first egg. There can therefore be a substantial difference in age between the first and fourth chick – something called asynchronous hatching. Most tawnies will use the same nest site (normally in a deciduous wood, a park or a large area of established gardens) year after year and, as long as food is available, they will remain resident in the same area. The eggs hatch after about thirty two days and the young remain at the nest site for about six weeks. Even when on the wing, young owls will remain with their parents for a further three months. A short break then follows before pairing and territory seeking takes place again in November when both sexes are very vocal. It is thought that tawny owls pair for life.

A fledgling tawny owl

They can change their nesting sites and roosting habits from time to time but, as yet, Mabel appears to be in no hurry to do either. Also unlike Mabel, many tawnies will choose to roost in ivy or against the bark of a tree. Tawny owls are brown or grey flecked with white and, against a tree trunk, this will give them a certain amount of camouflage. One way of locating a roosting tawny owl is to listen for a cacophony of sound created by smaller birds that have discovered its presence. Blackbirds in particular are very noisy when they discover such an owl and their commotion will attract others.

I viewed Mabel one morning being mobbed by a flock of eleven long-tailed tits. What a sight that made! These tiny birds fluttered around Mabel twittering away but she didn't even seem to blink. This charming flock of tits naturally attracted other birds and before long the party was joined by blackbirds, two mistle thrushes and later three jays. Despite the mistle thrush being a beautiful songster, when mobbing an owl it produced a long, rattling note. With that and the raucous jays it was a very noisy scene.

Thanks to mobbing birds I have discovered other tawny owls in Christchurch Park: I have seen one roosting in a holly bush near to the Reg Driver Visitor Centre and on several occasions I have discovered an owl in the holm oaks in the Wildlife Reserve. More often than not the owl will take little notice of these agitated songbirds. Mabel just sits there, mostly with her eyes closed, or perhaps occasionally looking down quite unconcerned at the people below.

Mabel being mobbed by a flock
of long-tailed tits

COMMON BARN OWL

The barn owl (*Tyto alba*) is undoubtedly the most popular of all our British owls. This is probably because it is distinctively white (at least from a distance) and flies very slowly with long wings over our fields and meadows, giving the watcher plenty of time to view this beautiful bird. Although it can appear white, in fact only its under parts are white: its back and upper parts are cream to golden brown mottled with grey and the top of its head is also mottled grey. The heart-shaped face is white, the eyes are black, the legs are long and the tail is short. Females are usually spotted on the under parts, particularly the breast. The males are far less spotted and I have cared for barn owls that are completely spot free.

Because it is a 'white' owl and flies silently, the barn owl has a ghostly appearance. It also has a large repertoire of eerie calls including a 'screech': perhaps it is little wonder that the bird has been associated with evil doings in English folklore. It has been called the 'demon owl' and even the 'death owl'. Lady Eveline Gurdon's 1893 *County Folk-lore: Suffolk* describes how the screech of an owl flying past the window of a sick person's room signified impending death!

The female barn owl incubates the clutch of white eggs, usually four to seven in number, although in captivity I have known clutches of up to fourteen. In the wild, barn owls will sometimes have two broods in one year but in captivity they might have three, or even four. The male's role is to bring food, mainly rats, voles and mice, to the nest. When disturbed at the nest, the female will hiss and click its beak as a deterrent. Sadly, when I was young, barn owls and other owls were often found on gamekeepers' gibbets – a very different sort of deterrent.

As youngsters, we boys would search for barn owls' nests. We would start by looking for pellets under holes in trees. Barn owl pellets are so distinctive, being black and shiny, quite unlike those of the tawny owl. We were never afraid of barn owls like we were of tawnies; barn owls always seemed quite delicate whereas tawnies are quite robust birds. I have never seen anything attack a tawny owl but on two occasions I have witnessed a barn owl under siege. Once, in a field at Shingle Street on the Suffolk coast, three noctule bats harassed a barn owl which was quartering a field at dusk, forcing the owl to the ground. On another occasion I saw a barn owl swoop down onto, I presume, a vole when it was attacked by a kestrel. Both birds grappled with each other for several minutes before flying off in opposite directions. I assume the vole was the reason for the 'fisticuffs' between these two birds but I don't know if it survived the contest.

It is difficult to ignore a barn owl when it is quartering a field or perched on a gatepost and, despite having kept wild disabled barn owls for many years I am always delighted when I see a barn owl in the wild. A couple of years ago in springtime, a pair of barn owls regularly hunted over a grassy field at Culpho near Ipswich. Surprisingly, they could be seen most mornings between 8am and 11am: yes, in broad daylight! It was not unusual to see a dozen cars parked by the roadside, with people on their way to work or school watching these birds systematically searching for prey. Barn owls will hunt in daylight if there is a shortage of rodents or if they have a large brood. I wonder how many motorists were late for work during that couple of weeks?

In the summer of 2012, I was asked to go to Tuddenham St Martin near Ipswich to visit Mrs Janet Welham who on several occasions had seen two barn owls quartering the fields near her home. Situated in a particularly beautiful part of Suffolk, these grass fields bordering the River Fynn are used for grazing a few horses and cattle. In the winter, because it is low lying, the area is often shrouded in mist, with temperatures several degrees lower than that of the surrounding countryside. Mrs Welham told me that the two owls had been seen regularly from 6am to mid-morning and again in the evening. She wanted to know why these owls were hunting together in daylight. I suggested that perhaps they had young and that prey was hard to come by or that their young were demanding more food. However, when I saw these owls, I changed my mind: I don't believe it was a pair of barn owls hunting, but rather an adult with an immature bird. The adult was very light in colour, almost white, whilst the other owl was much darker and, in a certain light, quite golden. Could it be possible that the adult was actually showing its youngster how to hunt? When young barn owls leave the nest do they automatically know how to search for their food? Perhaps parent barn owls must show their offspring how to search for and catch voles though of course this youngster may just have been following the adult bird in order to be first on the scene when prey was caught. Regardless of the cause, it was a wonderful sight that I know thrilled many others from Tuddenham and Ipswich.

Despite being less abundant than tawnies, the barn owl actually breeds much more readily in captivity. Encouraged by this, in the 1990's the Department of the Environment encouraged a breeding and release scheme to try to increase the nation's barn owl population. Authorised keepers bred barn owls in captivity and the young were released into areas considered suitable by the Wildlife Inspectorate. Keepers operating the scheme had their young barn owls ringed (but not with closed rings) so that future recoveries of the birds would indicate how far they had travelled and/or how they had died. However, the scheme was not a great success. For a start, not many of the youngsters stayed in the release area as barn owls (unlike tawnies) are great wanderers. Many starved and others were killed on the roads and railways. Very few young barn owls survived and the scheme was later abandoned although one barn owl ringed by me locally was recaptured in a building at Lowestoft some four years after its release.

The Suffolk Wildlife Trust is now at the forefront of barn owl conservation and, under the excellent stewardship of people like Steve Piotrowski, is using a more natural approach. Boxes are being erected in sites that are deemed suitable for barn owls but which currently have no, or few, nesting sites. The idea is that barn owls will breed in these boxes and thus numbers will increase. A statement from the Suffolk Wildlife Trust in January 2012 made clear its intentions: "Suffolk Wildlife Trust Barn Owl Advice focuses on land management and increasing nesting opportunities by installation of specially designed barn owl nest boxes targeting areas where there is suitable habitat. Those nesting in natural habitats – mostly hollow trees – cannot be persuaded to transfer to the nest boxes but their protégés regularly take to a new, less natural, home, and so the box design will be imprinted for generations to come."

According to Oka Last, Administrator of the Suffolk Community Barn Owl Project (a partnership between the Suffolk Wildlife Trust and the Suffolk Ornithologists' Group), "It is likely that there were more barn owls breeding in Suffolk in 2011 than at any time since the 1960's and perhaps even the 1930's. When the project started in 2006, there were about a hundred to a hundred and fifty pairs of barn owls breeding in the county but last year (2011) we identified twice that number." She confirmed that as East Suffolk has far more barn owls than West Suffolk the focus will now be on the west of the county.

Looking back at DEFRA's barn owl release scheme of the 1990's, I can honestly say that I think it was flawed. On reflection, it seems pointless to breed barn owls in captivity and then release them into the wild if so few will survive. The Suffolk Wildlife Trust and the Suffolk Ornithologists' Group have got it right. Of course, barn owl populations fluctuate depending on the availability of food. Bumper vole years produce more young barn owls. But even so it appears that the Suffolk Community Barn Owl Project is making a huge difference to one of Suffolk's most beautiful birds.

Adult little owl

LITTLE OWL

We have come to accept the little owl (*Athene noctua*) as a British species, but it is not so long ago that this delightful bird was absent from our shores. In the latter part of the nineteenth century, attempts were made by Lord Powys and others to establish little owls in our countryside by deliberately releasing them into the wild whilst others escaped from private collections. Perhaps Suffolk's little owls are descendants of the twenty or so birds released in Essex by Edmund Meade-Waldo at the end of the nineteenth century "to rid belfries of sparrows, bats and mice". Officially, however, the little owl – which really is little, being only about twenty-five centimetres in length – is now a British bird and I am certain that birdwatchers in this country love this small owl. It is always a pleasure to see one perching on a post 'bobbing' its head, and it is unthinkable to me that, just because it was previously released into the countryside deliberately, it should now be eradicated. The mandarin duck is also on the British list (which is managed by the British Ornithologists' Union) although, again, it is an 'alien' species: it too came from private collections. In my opinion both the little owl and the mandarin have done nothing but enhance our countryside.

The same cannot be said of some other animals that are to be found in the wild in the British Isles. The mink was once farmed for its fur but escapees, together with the deliberate malicious release by animal rights' groups, meant that many gained access to our streams and rivers to wreak havoc with our birds and small wild animals. It belongs to the weasel family and looks like a large, brown ferret. It is a ferocious killer and, despite concerted efforts to eradicate it, it is still at large. We cannot allow this animal to be included on the British list.

Another thriving alien species is the muntjac. This small, and in my opinion rather ugly, species of Asian deer is also an escapee from collections and zoos. It seems to breed throughout the year and has spread at an alarming rate. It damages trees and crops and is thought to be helping in the decline of the nightingale by eating and trampling down the scrub in which nightingales nest. So rapid is the spread of the muntjac that it can be found well within the boundaries of our towns and cities though is often overlooked because of its small size. It is probably far too late to try and eliminate this animal and, despite the damage that it causes, we must now accept it as a British wild animal.

This brings me to the grey squirrel. One of the very best places to study grey squirrels is our own Christchurch Park – unfortunately. This too is an alien in our country and is thought to be responsible for the decline of our native red squirrel. Young children may think of them as cute and cuddly, very tame and harmless looking but they are a pest taking the eggs and young of song birds. It is interesting to note that in areas of Cumbria and Northumberland the grey squirrel was successfully eradicated before the red squirrel was reintroduced, but it is now too late to exterminate this animal nationwide. Did you know that, as a non-native species, if you trap one, you are not allowed to release it back into the wild? What I do find remarkable about grey squirrels is their ability to migrate. I firmly believe that the squirrels in Christchurch Park travel to other areas of the town using the road systems. I often see dead squirrels along the Westerfield and Tuddenham Roads and I presume that these squirrels have been trying to seek pastures new after leaving Christchurch Park. Perhaps saturation point is reached even for the grey squirrels in our Park.

I have deviated somewhat from the little owl to discuss other escapees and introductions to our countryside. There are others, of course, but the little owl is here and we love it. From the fact that it is fairly tame, it seems to love us too (or at least likes being here). As its name implies, the little owl is our smallest owl. It has a broad flattened head and longish legs. It is brown, heavily speckled with white, with staring yellow eyes above which are white 'eyebrows'. When flying the little owl resembles the green woodpecker having an undulating flight with rapid wing beats alternating with gliding. More often than not, it is seen perched on a post or an exposed branch, often in broad daylight. It typically bobs its head, presumably in an attempt to focus on its prey. The call is a kind of 'meeu' repeated over and over again which seems to encourage other little owls to join in. They are partial to worms and beetles and will take small mammals and birds but, interestingly, of a large collection of little owl pellets that I once found under a nest hole, none contained any bones at all. Little owls nest in holes in trees but will also nest in buildings, particularly farm buildings. Although not native to this country, it is truly a very welcome addition.

A friend of mine, Don Gostling, worked on the land for many years, especially in the Grundisburgh and Kesgrave areas. He says that when he was ploughing he would often see little owls perched on bare branches or posts watching him work. The reason, says Don, was obvious: little owls love worms and periodically would fly from their perches and pounce on those that the plough had uncovered, often in the company of black-headed gulls.

There are several pairs in the area of arable land interspersed with farm buildings around my studio – a typical little owl habitat. One pair regularly nests in an old walnut tree and in late summer, when the ground (clay) is baked hard, the little owls sit in a family group on posts searching for ground beetles. I have not seen little owls take birds but, when the family are exposed on their posts, the local blackbirds mob the owls mercilessly.

A pair of adult little owls with three owlets

SHORT-EARED OWL

Every autumn short-eared owls (*Asio flammeus*) arrive in Suffolk on migration from Scandinavia, Iceland and Russia. They sometimes appear in large numbers but usually they reach our shores in ones or twos. They fly in northwards over Landguard Point near Felixstowe, the most southerly point in Suffolk, normally just above the water. I have also seen them arrive at East Lane, Shingle Street, Orfordness and Aldeburgh usually being harried by herring gulls as they come in before dropping down into vegetation. They are daytime fliers and in the winter you are almost guaranteed to see one or more on the marshes and fields at Shingle Street.

The autumn of 2011 was an especially productive time for incoming short-eared owls and we even added one to the list of birds seen in Christchurch Park, Ipswich. Early one morning, forty carrion crows and jackdaws mobbing a clearly exhausted short-eared owl caused a loud commotion over northern Ipswich. Try as it might, the owl found it difficult to escape from the excited corvids. Slowly, the flock of birds drifted south with the owl weaving and diving in its bid to rid itself of the frenzied mob. It was several minutes before the crows lost interest and the owl could glide down into the Park in search of cover and peace.

The short-eared owl has a huge geographical range, being found in both the new and old worlds. It is a medium sized owl being approximately thirty six centimetres in length and it is coloured creamy brown with dark brown streaks on the breast and dark brown bars on wings and tail. The long wings have dark brown/black 'wrists' on both the upper and undersides. Being a daytime flier, the eyes are yellow (night-flying owls tend to have orange eyes) but they are

Short-eared owls

made more pronounced by being surrounded by black feathered edgings.

The short-eared owl, as its name implies, is so called because of the feathered tufts on its head, which are much smaller than those of its relative, the long-eared owl. This owl is a bird of open countryside and because of this it nests on the ground, usually in rough grassland. A few pairs nest in East Anglia but, as I have already indicated, numbers are greatly reinforced in autumn and winter. Egg laying begins in late April or May when up to eight eggs are produced. The female, as with other species of owl, does the incubation and the eggs hatch after about twenty-six days. The female and the young are fed with rodents (especially voles) hunted down and caught by the male.

*Migrating short-eared owl arriving at
East Lane, Bawdsey, Suffolk*

LONG-EARED OWL

The long-eared owl (*Asio otus* formerly *Strix otus*) is similar in size to the tawny owl being about thirty four centimetres in length but it is essentially a night owl – though I will soon give examples that contradict this. It is coloured brown, streaked all over with dark brown and black. As a 'night owl' it has orange eyes, and it has quite large ear tufts on the top of its head. They are called ear tufts but in fact they have nothing to do with its ears; they are feathered tufts used for display, the ears being on the side of the head. There are two hundred and twenty species of owl of which about fifty have tufts. The undersides of the wings show black markings on the 'wrist', but the markings are not as prominent as those of the short-eared owl.

The long-eared owl has been described in appearance as a smaller version of the eagle owl – I suppose this is mostly because of its orange eyes and ear tufts. The other main likeness is that the species have similar threat displays: they both spread out their wings and raise their back feathers in an aggressive posture. But there the similarity ends. The long-eared owl is a bird of conifer forests and mature, dense woodland. Its call is a treble 'oooo' although the fledged young produce a noise that has been described as a rusty gate closing. The chosen nest site, often in a coniferous tree where four to six eggs are laid, is usually an old crow's nest or a disused squirrel's drey. The female does the incubation and eggs hatch at about twenty six days. The male provides the food, mainly rodents.

Some years ago, a pair regularly nested in woodland on Martlesham Heath near Ipswich. This was after the RAF abandoned the area but before houses were built. The nesting site was a former crow's nest and young were successfully raised. At night in the summer the calls of the adults and the youngsters' 'rusty gate' calls could be heard from quite a distance. In the same area there was also a winter roost in some tangled gorse bushes for at least half a dozen long-eared owls – communal winter roosting is an unusual feature of this particular species of owl. Surprisingly, the roost was only a few feet off the ground. It was not known if this roost was of resident or migrant birds.

In the early days of the Suffolk Ornithologists' Group, members had a day's outing in early summer to the Brecklands on the border of Norfolk and Suffolk. Reports had been received of an owl hunting during daylight and we were anxious to find out more. The Brecks is a rather lovely, barren area of large stony fields bordered with rows of Scots pine (it is one of the driest places in England). By the time we arrived, the sun was shining brightly and it was very

warm. Sure enough the owl duly appeared, slowly flapping its way across the field before settling onto a post. With tufts held aloft, this long-eared owl surveyed us all imperiously. It remained perched there for many minutes before flying around in a large circle and coming back to the same spot. Once more it launched itself and for some time it quartered the ground, flying with long, deliberate wing beats, clearly showing its lighter under parts and black 'wrist' markings. The watching SOG party assumed that the long-eared owl was hunting for food in daylight as it was probably supporting some very hungry youngsters.

To see a long-eared owl lazily gliding or slowly flapping its wings could give the impression that speed is not part of its make-up. However, that would be totally wrong. The long-eared owl, as with other owls, is a killer capable of surprising its victims with exceptional speed.

One of the early SOG bulletins reported on a case in Cheshire where one of our members was watching a long-eared owl perched on a post on the edge of a conifer plantation near Macclesfield. Again, this was in daylight and it appeared to be 'snoozing', that was until a pair of jays discovered the sleepy owl. The quietness of a pleasant day was broken by the raucous behaviour of the jays as they began continually harassing the owl. It just sat there, ear tufts erect, immobile. Then in a flash the long-eared owl suddenly launched itself and attacked one of the jays, which fell to the ground dead. The owl (perhaps surprisingly) just returned to its post. The other jay flew off – very quietly!

The British population of long-eared owls is swelled in autumn and winter by migratory birds from northern Europe. Whereas short-eared owls tend to come to these shores by day, long-eared owls usually arrive in darkness. However, I have seen long-eared owls coming in during daylight and, on one occasion at East Lane, near Bawdsey, short-eared owls were arriving just above the waves whilst circling above them was a solitary long-eared owl.

MRS GOUDY AND THE HAWK OWL

This extraordinary episode began in the autumn of 1982 when my good friend, John Goudy, a woodsman and countryman from Foxhall near Ipswich, telephoned me to report a bird which had taken up residence at his mother's house. Mrs Rene Goudy lived in an isolated cottage on the Broxtead Estate at Sutton Heath, near Woodbridge. The surrounding land near Mrs Goudy's house was a mixture of farmland, ancient woods and heathland. Sheep grazed some of the fields. John thought that the bird in question that had taken to roosting in his mother's porch was a sparrowhawk. Whilst this report was quite interesting it was, after all, just a sparrowhawk, so that was that. I did not even bother to pay Mrs Goudy a visit.

Four months after John's initial telephone call, I received another. "Reg, that sparrowhawk is still roosting in my mum's porch but, strangely, it has the face of an owl." I nearly dropped the phone in my excitement. I told John that I would go and visit his mother that very afternoon. By the time I reached the Broxtead Estate, it was late afternoon. I introduced myself to Mrs Goudy and explained that I had come to see her 'sparrowhawk' roosting in her porch. Rene Goudy explained that I was too early to see her guest so she would make me a cup of tea. Apparently, the bird only arrived at its roost just as the light was failing. "If we look out of this window", Mrs Goudy said, "we will be able to see the bird as it makes its way to my house through the sheep in that field." I did not really know what to make of this; it all seemed a bit surreal.

I finished my cup of tea. Suddenly Mrs Goudy cried "Here it comes!" There, flying very low to the ground was this greyish brown, long-tailed bird, zigzagging its way between the sheep. Over the fence, across the garden and up to the porch it flew. "I suggest that we have another cup of tea, dear, to give the bird time to settle down and then we'll go and have a chat with it." What? Did Rene really mean this? Did she really intend that we would go cup in hand and actually talk to this bird? "I always have a little word with it." Excitedly, I started on my second cup of tea…

Midway through our drink, Mrs Goudy suggested that it was time to go and view the bird as it had now probably settled down for the night. So, taking our tea with us, we went into the porch. By now it was dark and my host produced a torch from her pinafore. "Hello darling", she began, and then carried on chatting, not to a sparrowhawk but to a hawk owl! Yes, a northern hawk owl. I had never even seen one and I do not think that a hawk owl had ever been recorded in Suffolk before. This is a bird of the sub-arctic but in severe winters it can travel further south, often being quite unafraid of humans. This would explain why Mrs Goudy's owl was quite willing to be 'chatted up'.

In the Northern Hemisphere, the hawk owl (*Surnia ulula*) is found from the temperate coniferous forests to the sub-arctic. It gets its name from the fact that, with its long tail, it resembles a hawk, particularly when in flight. However, that is its only connection to a hawk. It is very much an owl, of medium size (thirty six to forty five centimetres), with a small facial disc of whitish grey, boldly marked with a black outer edge. The eyes are yellow and quite small. The crown of its head is mottled black and white with a dark V shape on the back of its neck. The back of the bird is chequered in dark brown and white. The wings are long, narrow, pointed and barred, as is the long tail. The breast and under parts are whitish barred with black. Unusually for owls, the hawk owl is diurnal.

After a while, we left the owl in peace but, before I left the Broxtead Estate, I was introduced to the gamekeeper who had also seen the bird. He asked how many birders would arrive in the morning if news of a hawk owl in Suffolk were to become public knowledge: about two thousand, I replied. He warned me that if I let the cat (or perhaps owl) out of the bag then the bird might well disappear, and he also wasn't keen on people trespassing on his land. Therefore I kept the experience to myself.

Later that week I was told that the owl had ceased coming to its roost in the porch. I like to think that this wonderfully attractive owl had journeyed back to its breeding quarters in Russia or northern Scandinavia. I visited dear Rene once more and saw the roost site in daylight. All that remained was a white splashed wall and a large pile of pellets. What a fantastic birding experience this had been and one that, because of my original apathy, had so nearly been missed. Luckily, like a true birder, I made notes at the time and, even on reading these notes now, it all seems a bit unreal. Come on, how many rarities such as this get to be talked to, at such close quarters, by a dear old lady holding a cup of tea?

Footnote: Rene Goudy this year (2012) celebrated her 98th birthday.

An eagle owl, the most powerful of all the owls

EAGLE OWL

The Eurasian eagle owl (*Bubo bubo*) was occasionally found in this country until the end of the nineteenth century when it was eradicated – thanks to man. It had to be man as the eagle owl has no predators apart from man who seems capable of shooting, trapping or poisoning any wild creature. Even today our most regal and most magnificent birds of prey are being persecuted despite the laws designed to protect them.

Most reported sightings must have been false however as officially the eagle owl has been extinct in Britain for thousands of years. Why it should be missing here is a bit of a mystery as it is present in some numbers as close as the Netherlands. Occasionally pairs of eagle owls are reported to have bred in this country, with some claiming that these are wild birds that have found their way here from the continent. I very much doubt that. Instead I think it is possible that these birds have escaped from captivity (there are probably over three thousand captive eagle owls) or pairs might even have been released just in order to be filmed.

My first experience with an eagle owl was when I was sent a youngster from Wales. Paul Llewellyn was a fellow DEFRA Wildlife Inspector who also kept birds of prey. He was quite willing to let me have one of his captive-bred eagle owlets to study and so one was delivered to me by courier. It arrived in a large cardboard box originally designed for bananas! The box was covered with netting and a message that warned the driver all hell would be let loose if he removed it. When the eagle owlet arrived it was an ugly thing: large staring eyes, huge feet, very few feathers and covered in down. And it was hungry. It immediately devoured two chicks and then adopted a 'threat' display which I quickly came to associate with all eagle owls. The youngster grew rapidly and when it gained its feathers its threat displays became even more spectacular. By this time it was housed in a large aviary and, when annoyed, it would puff out its feathers, open its wings and make loud clicking noises with its bill.

Being a Wildlife Inspector specialising in birds of prey meant that I visited many keepers who, inevitably, had surplus owls, some of which came my way. Others I rescued after they had escaped from captivity. One eagle owl I remember had somehow managed to get into a chicken run but after devouring all the chickens couldn't extricate itself. I was asked to catch the bird. The obvious way was to throw a large net over the owl but, unfortunately, no such net was available. So I decided to position myself behind the eagle owl and, when it was not looking, grab its legs. Simple! I don't think so... I had just one chance for, if I failed to grab its legs, I would receive severe lacerations (or worse) to my hands. Fortunately luck was on my side, and I emerged from the chicken run with one enormous – and extremely angry – eagle owl hanging upside down from my hands.

So there are no eagle owls in the wild in this country. Well, not one that has arrived under its own steam. However, eagle owls do escape and others are deliberately set free. Eagle owls can breed successfully in Britain, particularly if there is a good food supply but an escaped eagle owl can cause havoc to the local wildlife. It will kill and eat more or less anything that moves, although it prefers rabbit. Some years ago, one such bird set up home in a quarry at Great Blakenham in Suffolk where it systematically ate the wildlife starting with rabbits and then jackdaws. The jackdaws were nesting in holes in the sides of the quarry and the eagle owl would wait for the corvids to leave their nest, then launch itself and grab them in flight. For such a large bird, it was very agile. Being at the top of the food chain and having no natural predators there is very little that eagle owls will not tackle, especially at night. This one was eventually captured in the village after the local cats began to disappear…

The eagle owlet arrived in a large cardboard box...

The eagle owl is one of the largest of all owls, being sixty to seventy centimetres in length. The female can be considerable larger than the male. There are twelve species of *bubo* and together they have a huge geographical range though they are replaced in the Arctic by the snowy owl and in Australia by hawk owls. They also vary in size, though the largest and most powerful is the Eurasian eagle owl, *Bubo bubo*, which has ear tufts and I suppose could vaguely be described as looking like an enormous long-eared owl. It is very strong, barrel shaped and mostly brown in colour, heavily streaked with darker brown. The throat is white. Like the long-eared owl, the eyes are orange. The feet are feathered. The Eurasian eagle owl ranges from the Arctic Circle to southern Europe and it nests on rocky outcrops, in caves, large holes in trees and on the ground. One nest was even found on a football pitch (disused of course). It will willingly use the old nests of an eagle and often rotates its nest site. Two to six eggs are laid but three or four are more usual. Egg laying begins early in February or March and the eggs take thirty five days to hatch. As with most owls and birds of prey, incubation begins after the first or second egg is laid. Therefore there can be quite a large difference in age and size of the young produced. The male is responsible for providing the food for the female and the young whilst at the nest site, which can consist of almost any wildlife including hedgehogs. The young leave the nest at five to six weeks. A larger eagle owlet will sometimes eat its smaller sibling – a case of survival of the fittest!

The call of the eagle owl sounds very much likes its Latin name, 'bubo bubo', or rather 'oooo-oooo', and can carry over four to five miles. I have heard an eagle owl calling at night in southern France on a very warm evening, a sound that seemed to float over the countryside.

SNOWY OWL

Snowy owls (*Bubo scandiacus*, formerly known as *Nyctea scandiaca*) have become very popular following the *Harry Potter* films when they played a leading role alongside Daniel Radcliffe. Although Harry's owl Hedwig is apparently female, only male snowy owls are white and so the seven birds that played the part in the movies were all males. Unfortunately, when the snowy owl was not flying or 'being magic', it spent most of its time in a cage designed to house a parrot. Not an ideal way in which to show off this magnificent owl, in my opinion.

In the wild, the snowy owl is a wondrous bird. It is between fifty three and sixty five centimetres in height with the female being larger and heavier than the male. Some males are completely white, whilst others show just a few black or brown markings. Although the female is mostly white she is heavily marked with black, including the crown of her head. The eyes of both male and female are yellow and the bill and talons are black. Snowy owls tend to be barrel-shaped: in other words when standing on the ground they appear to be rather bulky. They do not have visible ear tufts.

When not starring in *Harry Potter* films, snowy owls are found in the tundra above the Arctic Circle where they nest on the ground, often on a hummock with a good view of the surrounding area. They feed on lemmings (in a good lemming year they can eat upwards of sixteen hundred of them), voles and birds. Like all owls, the amount of chicks raised depends on the availability of food and when food is abundant they will raise double the normal amount of three or four young. Snowy owls are very rare migrants to the British Isles but in the 1960's a pair successfully raised young on the island of Fetlar in the Shetlands. They can survive up to forty days without eating, but when food is in short supply in the winter, snowy owls will often migrate south and in Canada they can be found on open agricultural land and even at airports. I have a Canadian friend who lives in the industrial town of Hamilton, Ontario, who relates that in one severe winter, thousands of snowy owls migrated south. He even found one in his back garden.

Because they are ground nesting birds, Arctic foxes and skuas prey upon the eggs and young. The owls have no real defence against foxes, and so adult birds will feign injury in an effort to lure the fox away from the nest site. Owlets have grey downy feathers which absorb sunshine and help to camouflage them against predators.

Snowy owls are popular birds to have in a bird of prey collection: they look cuddly and endearing. But, like all owls, they can be quite fearsome – they devour most of their prey whole and head first. They have a threat display that is similar to other large owls such as the eagle owl: they spread out their wings, puff up their feathers and click their bills. In 1981 I was keeping a pair of snowy owls for a friend when we had severe gales. The winds were so ferocious that the roof of the aviary was completely blown away. The snowy owls, however, took very little notice and remained together on their perch until a new roof was put in place.

Snowy owls may now be only a circumpolar bird, but some fourteen thousand years ago, when the Arctic climate extended much further south, one of our forebears painted an image of a pair of snowy owls with chicks onto the walls of a cave in Ariège, in the French Pyrenees. This is considered to be the first depiction of a recognisable bird species in art – and quite an inspiration for those of us who follow after.

*A pair of snowy owls, the female on
the nest*

WHERE TO SEE OWLS IN SUFFOLK

For the birdwatcher or owl enthusiast, Suffolk is a county where you can see all five of the native British species of owl in the wild (there are over two hundred species listed worldwide). Little owls can be spotted by day year round. In autumn and winter, short-eared owls are active on coastal marshland, again during daylight hours. But to see long-eared owls I suppose the Brecks or any large coniferous forest is the place. However, they are mainly night owls. Then there is the tawny owl – not least Mabel, our 'star' tawny owl of national fame, who has been viewed sitting in her oak tree by so many visitors to Christchurch Park, Ipswich over the last four years.

According to the Suffolk Wildlife Trust, barn owls can be seen at many of their sites, particularly those in the Waveney Valley. There are at least a dozen nesting pairs around Carleton and Castle Marshes and more at Oulton Marshes. They are resident in the habitats surrounding the Alde/Ore/Butley estuary and frequent visitors to the Trust's marshland reserves at Darsham, Sizewell, Hazlewood and Snape Marshes. In 2012 a rather wonderful innovation was the Trust's live streaming from a camera inside a barn owl nest box at their Redgrave and Lopham Fen reserve. This innovative and informative scheme was supported by Barnes Construction who have also helped to build owl boxes to the Trust's bespoke design.

For those who would like the assurance of seeing owls in captivity, then the Suffolk Owl Sanctuary at Stonham Barns is a must. There you will find not only British birds but owls from all over the world, including great grey, spectacled, boobook, Ural and Asian wood owls. You can see eagle owls from Asia, Europe and Africa and the equivalent eagle owl – the great horned owl – from North America. The Sanctuary is home to more than one snowy owl. You can observe owls at close quarters and maybe even touch one. Even more excitingly, they put on flying displays so that as well as seeing 'static' owls you will see these magnificent creatures in flight If you think that *Bubo bubo* looks large when sitting on a perch, then you must experience it looking even mightier when swooping down right over your head!

Owls very sadly do get run over. Too often we see a carcass of a barn owl or a mangled corpse of a tawny owl lying by the roadside. All owls will scavenge and where better to find an easy meal than on the road? Unfortunately, owls are blinded by car lights and are not quick enough to avoid fast-moving vehicles. Tawny owls, in particular, fall victim, especially in the breeding season when they mistakenly think that other road kills such as rats, birds and insects, are easy pickings.

Finally, if you want to see owls that have been mounted (more dead owls...) then the Ipswich Museum is the place to visit. The Ogilvie Collection houses some of the very finest examples of birds in glass cases – taxidermy at its best. Fergus Menteith Ogilvie was born in 1861 in Kensington, studied at Cambridge University and became an ophthalmic surgeon. As well as being a noted ornithologist he also grew orchids, for which he gained the RHS Gold medal. He collected all the birds in the collection himself (at a time when there was ignorance of the effect this might have on the various species) from Suffolk as well as from the Ogilvie Estate in Argyllshire, Scotland. The birds were either shot or trapped, and collected both for educational purposes as well as to add to his personal collection.

From 1902 the collection was housed at The Wardens, a purpose-built private museum on the Sizewell Estate near Leiston. Underfloor heating, remote-controlled roof louvres, overhead glazed lights and individually controlled roller blinds protected the specimens from ultra-violet rays. When Fergus' widow, the Lady Marion Ogilvie, donated the collection to the Ipswich Museum in 1918, it consisted of two hundred and thirty five cases of seven hundred and seventy specimens of one hundred and ninety seven different species.

The birds were mounted by Thomas Edward Gunn who was born in 1844 in Norwich. He studied under John Sayer in the city and later became probably the greatest British taxidermist. Whatever one's feelings about taxidermy, the birds are undeniably very beautifully mounted. Gunn not only knew his birds well but he was also a very capable artist. Each glass case has a hand-painted background suggestive of the bird's habitat.

Taxidermy has changed over the years. Now, of course, all taxidermists have to be registered with DEFRA. Work on protected species has to be notified to DEFRA with a subsequent visit by a Wildlife Inspector. Most birds now are either road kills or come from falconers. If any inspector is in doubt over the way that the specimens were obtained, then the bird is removed to a veterinary clinic for x-ray and examination. No mounted bird can be sold without an authentication certificate. If the taxidermist is found guilty of having illegally taken specimens from the wild then a heavy fine or even imprisonment can be imposed.

EPILOGUE

In my formative years I was hugely influenced by the great botanist and conservationist Francis Simpson. He was very much an individual despite spending all his working life, from 1930 to 1977, as a keeper of the Natural History Department at the Ipswich Museum. As a small boy I would collect specimens of wildlife – insects, caterpillars, water creatures and other wiggly things including snakes – and on Saturday mornings I would take these wonderful creatures, all secure in my Mickey Mouse gas mask holder, for Mr Simpson to inspect. He would name and describe their life cycle for me and generally guide my naturalist ambitions in the right direction.

After a number of years away I became reacquainted with Francis Simpson. He was very interested in the fact that I was rehabilitating disabled wild owls and was surprised at the number of owls that came to grief for one reason or another. Although his main interest was flora, he was fascinated by all forms of wildlife, including my owls. My most rewarding memory of Francis was of meeting him in 'no-man's land'. Let me explain. Many years ago marsh harriers were beginning to increase in number in Suffolk but were still pretty rare. I had discovered one nest in a dyke in fields at Bawdsey and another in a field of rye a short distance away. Both nests contained four youngsters; the field was large and the rye was high. Whilst sketching these young birds, I noticed a head coming towards me above the rye. Despite the intense heat, the head was wearing a woolly hat! It was Francis. Our heads met. I showed Francis the nest and he was overjoyed. We walked back to the village together where I got on my bike and he caught a bus back to Ipswich. Francis was a truly amazingly dedicated naturalist. Every time we met he was courteous and always interested to discover what I had seen. I held Francis in the highest esteem alongside another great man, Herbert Axell, whose name is synonymous with the Minsmere Nature Reserve.

In the 1960's I was a RSPB representative for East Suffolk when I first met Bert Axell at Minsmere. Many more visits followed when I would be handed a shovel and persuaded to help with creating 'the scrape', the huge shallow lagoon dotted with islands that we dug out of the marshland. At that time Bert had full use of one workable old tractor which he allowed my young daughter to drive. Whilst working at Minsmere in those early days I would assist Bert in the trapping of coypus – large, South American rodents which had escaped from captivity. These animals had set up camp on the reserve and were damaging the dykes. One had even taken a partial liking to the scrape where it sat on clutches of avocet eggs. We captured the coypus and Bert dealt with them. Bert and his wife Joan were very hospitable. In the summer they loved to entertain their guests on the shore adjacent to the reserve, feeding them plates of chicken sandwiches. Later Bert would joke that the coypus that he had trapped were skinned and stored in his freezer – and that the 'chicken' sandwiches I had devoured were actually coypu sandwiches! Was he really joking?

Although Bert was fascinated that I was trying to save disabled wild owls he regularly pointed out that he was not in favour of birds in cages. His attitude was that if a bird was found with a broken wing or leg, no matter how perfect the mend was, that bird would never be the same when released back into the wild. He firmly believed that an accident of that proportion was far too traumatic for the bird to make a complete recovery. Although he had a great love of owls and birds of prey he would fiercely defend his avocets that nested on the scrape and occasionally a tawny owl or kestrel might go the same way as a marauding fox...

Bert could, on occasion, be somewhat cantankerous and he did not suffer fools gladly. However he was always charming to the ladies, and courteous and friendly to me. The work that Bert carried out for the RSPB was prodigious and it was his plans to save the bittern that are largely responsible for the bird's rise in fortune. Bert's expertise was not only reserved for Minsmere. After gaining a Churchill Fellowship, Bert travelled the world advising on bird conservation. I well remember standing in a reed bed at Minsmere with Bert and Eric Hosking, the late, great bird photographer who lost his left eye in an attack by a tawny owl and who wittily entitled his autobiography *An Eye for a Bird*. For hours we waited in vain as we tried to photograph bearded tits. We took no photographs, but listening to Bert and Eric telling tales of their bird encounters was enthralling.

The Suffolk Ornithologists' Group has gone from strength to strength since its formation in 1973. In addition to its work with barn owls, it is now recognised as the foremost bird-recording organisation in the county and it maintains strong ties with RSPB Minsmere, the Suffolk Wildlife Trust, Landguard Bird Observatory and the Suffolk Naturalists' Society. This is a far cry from all those years ago when a small group of like-minded birders from both the east and west of Suffolk first came together. Initially, for obvious reasons, the SOG was divided into east and west but for the benefit of publishing a bulletin we would meet to discuss recent sightings, the results of surveys and to suggest future plans. From the start, we realised that surveys and records were important. We conducted a cuckoo survey, one on mute swans, another on the kestrel and also one on the nightjar, but by far our most outstanding survey was 'The Rook Survey' of the mid 1970's. This had not been done before and so we had to start from scratch. Our members divided Suffolk into squares and each member was given an area in which to count rooks' nests. Rooks are early nesters and so their nests are easy to see before the leaves appear on the trees. The total number of nests was counted and the results were published in a book entitled *The Rook in Suffolk.* What is so special about this is that all future rook surveys carried out have something with which to compare and *The Rook in Suffolk* is used not only as a comparison but also as a guide as to how a survey might be conducted. This proved to be a great boost for the SOG.

When members from east and west Suffolk met in those early days, it was agreed that the SOG would benefit from the publication of a bi-monthly bulletin so that members would be informed as to what birds had been recently recorded. There were only a few of us in those early days. It was hard work for Robin Hopper, Mike Jeanes and Ken Carlisle from west Suffolk and Mike Hall, Don Nesling and me in the east to sift through members' reported sightings and to compile an interesting bulletin. Out of our own pockets we bought a second-hand Gestetner printing machine, reams of foolscap paper and gallons of ink. The bulletin was usually run off on my dining table. In the beginning it was crude and, compared to today's beautifully produced bulletins, our first efforts must appear similar to (and almost as ancient as) the Dead Sea scrolls. But at least we made the effort. The records of sightings, although unverified, are recorded for all to see and of course they are an important benchmark as to the status of birds in Suffolk some forty years ago. Many of the original members of the SOG are sadly no longer with us but the contributions they made to the Group at its conception were so very important.

I am glad to say that one of the co-founders, Mike Hall, still does a bit of bird watching when he can. Robin Hopper has moved 'up north' but regularly comes back to Suffolk to visit his old birding friends. Mike Jeanes is resident in Ipswich and remains an active birdwatcher and I am still making notes, writing articles and sketching the same species of birds (including owls) that I sketched in 1973. Some of us, wisely or not, are still dedicated to the cause. I like to think that the formation of the Suffolk Ornithologists' Group was a huge encouragement to the likes of Philip Murphy and Mike Marsh and to all those others who today keep their eyes and ears open to the extraordinary birdlife that is all around us.

Even in those early days of the SOG, members regularly visited my studio not only to see my artwork but also to view the tawny owls that I was attempting to rehabilitate. Everyone was fascinated to see them all perched in a row in the aviary. As visitors walked the length of the enclosure, so the owls' eyes would follow them. It always amused me, as I sat working, to see all the owls' heads turning in unison as the people passed by.

These owls raised our spirits – just as Mabel does for so many of us today.

OWL TERMINOLOGY

Here are some explanations of words that you might come across when reading about owls:

Altricial Baby owls are altricial, which means that they are helpless when hatched. The opposite of **precocial**, when young are relatively mature and mobile.

Asynchronous hatching This is when eggs in a clutch hatch over a number of days. It appears to have evolved as a strategy for raising the largest number of young allowed by the current resources of food. Incubation begins before the laying of the last egg. Those hatching first will have a head start and younger chicks may struggle to survive.

Classification Owls belong to the order *Strigiformes*. This is further divided into *Strigidae* ('typical owls', for example the tawny owl) and *Tytonidae* (barn owl).

Closed ring A numbered metal ring placed on a young bird to denote that it has been bred in captivity.

Crepuscular Active primarily at twilight, either at dawn or dusk. Compare with **diurnal** (active during the day) and **nocturnal** (active at night).

Dimorphism This means the occurrence of two distinct forms in a species. In tawny owls, there are two forms, grey and brown. In birds males are typically larger than females but many owls exhibit reverse **sexual dimorphism** in size – ie the female is larger than the male.

Fledging This is the period between hatching and leaving the nest. Some birds vacate the nest within a few hours of hatching but it is usually a few weeks before owls can fly. Like other birds, owls are called **nestlings** while they are still in the nest and **fledglings** when they acquire their flight feathers and can start to fly. Owlets pass through a phase called **branching** when they can jump and flutter about in trees and sometimes on the ground (they are usually quite adept at climbing back up again).

Gibbet line A collection of dead animals and birds traditionally strung up on wires by gamekeepers to exhibit what 'vermin' (including owls) had been destroyed.

Incubation Sitting upon eggs for the purpose of hatching.

Migration Most owls don't migrate, staying pretty much in the same area all their lives. An exception is the snowy owl.

Mobbing An attack on one bird by a group of (often smaller) birds. The reasons for this are not entirely clear.

Monogamy Owls stay faithful to one partner throughout their lives and so are described as **monogamous**.

Owlet A baby owl. Occasionally also used for some of the smallest owl species.

Parliament The commonly accepted collective noun for a group of owls. Other terms used include bazaar, congress, diss, stare, wisdom and sagaciousness. Some more specific collective nouns include silence (when in flight), stable (barn owls), volery (little owls) and blizzard (snowy owls).

Pellets Owls either tear off chunks from their prey or eat them whole. The acids in their digestive system then liquefy everything except the feathers, bones or fur and these undigested parts are compacted and disposed of via the owl's mouth, roughly one pellet for each animal consumed. The larger the owl, the larger the size of pellet. Owls need to regurgitate to remain healthy as the process of the pellet moving through the digestive system helps to remove harmful bacteria. Other birds that produce pellets include kingfishers, flycatchers, herons and hawks.

Pole trap An illegal method of trapping owls and birds of prey by placing a spring trap on top of a perching post.

Quartering A method of hunting used by barn owls, slowly flying back and forth over an open area, often at a low level.

Raptor A bird of prey such as an eagle, owl, hawk or falcon. From the Latin "to seize and carry off".

Red List A list of endangered birds and animals in need of special protection, officially the International Union for Conservation of Nature Red List of Threatened Species.

Remiges and rectrices Flight feathers on wings are called remiges. The longer flight feathers are called **primaries** and the smaller ones **secondaries**. Rectrices lie at the rear edge of the tail and help the bird to steer and brake.

Scavenge To search for and take discarded material, ie food. Owls primarily hunt but also sometimes scavenge.

Territory A chosen area in which owls, or other species of birds, hunt and breed.

Zygodactyl The structure of owls' feet, where two toes face forwards and two back (one of which may rotate 180 degrees when required), enabling them to easily grasp their prey.

WILDLIFE INDEX
Numbers in bold indicate an illustration

Asian wood owl, 60
Avocet, 64, 65
Barn owl, common, 22, **30**, 31-35, **35**, 60, 61, 65, 68, 69, 70
Bat, 32, 37
Bearded tit, 65, 72
Beetle, 39, 40
Bittern, 65
Blackbird, 28, 40
Black-headed gull, 39
Boobook owl, 60
Budgerigar, 20
Butterfly, 3
Caterpillar, 63
Common barn owl, *see* Barn owl
Coypu, 64, 72
Crow, 41, 45
Cuckoo, 65
Dog, 4, 8
Eagle, 9, 22, 56, 70
Eagle owl, 45, **52**, 53-56, **55**, 58, 60-61
Earthworm, 9, 39
Falcon, **20**, 22, **23**, 70
Ferret, 37
Fish, 1
Flycatcher, 70
Fox, 8, 9, 58, 65
Golden eagle, 22
Gorse, 46
Goshawk, 22
Great grey owl, 60
Great horned owl, 61
Green woodpecker, 39
Grey squirrel, 8, 9, 38
Hawk, 9, 50, 70
Hawk owl, **48**, 49-51, **50**, 56
Hedgehog, 19, 56
Hen harrier, 23
Heron, 70
Herring gull, 9, 41
Holly, 28
Holm oak, 28
Hornet, 2
Ivy, 28
Jackdaw 41, 54
Jay, 28, 47
Kestrel, 18, 32, 65
Kingfisher, 70
Lemming, 57

Lesser black-backed gull, 9
Little owl, **36**, 37-40, **40**, 60, 69
Long-eared owl, 43, **44**, 45-47, 56, 60
Long-tailed tit, 28, **29**
Mabel, 1, 3, 5-6, **7**, 8-10, 11-14, **15**, **16**, 25-28, **29**, 60, 67, **67**
Mallard, 9
Mandarin duck, 25, 37
Marsh harrier, 63, 72
Merlin, 22, 23
Mink, 37
Mistle thrush, 28
Mole, 9, 19
Mouse, 9, 10, 11, 19, 31, 37
Muntjac, 38
Mute swan, 25, 65
Nightingale, 38
Nightjar, 66
Noctule bat, 32
Oak, 1, 3, 4, 5, 13, 28, 60
Osprey, 1
Owl, *see individual species*
Parrot, 20, 57
Peregrine falcon, *see* Falcon
Pheasant, 11
Rabbit, 9, 54
Rat, 1, 8, 9, 10, 11, 19, 31, 61
Red-backed shrike, 72
Rook, 66
Scots pine, 46
Short-eared owl, 19, 41-43, **42**, **43**, 45, 47, 60
Shrew, 9
Skua, 58
Snake, 63
Snowy owl, 26, 56, 57-58, **59**, 61, 69
Sparrow, 37
Sparrowhawk, 49, 50, *see also* Hawk
Spectacled owl, 60
Squirrel, 8, 9, 38, 45
Stoat, 19
Tawny owl, 1, 3-6, **7**, 8-10, **10**, 11-14, **15**, **16**, 17, **24**, 25-28, **27**, **29**, 32-34, 45, 60, 61, 65, 67, 68
Ural owl, 60
Vole, 31, 32, 33, 35, 43, 57
Walnut, 40
Weasel, 19, 37
Woodpecker, 39

ABOUT THE AUTHOR

Reg Snook's interest in wildlife was fostered in the years following the Second World War when the countryside was a wonderful place in which a young boy could roam. This led to a lifelong interest in wildlife and a love of birds.

Reg and his family moved to the Christchurch Park area of Ipswich over forty years ago. Since then he has been keeping records of all the bird life in the Park, culminating in his hugely popular first book, *Portrait of a Park: a year with the wildlife of Christchurch Park*. In the late sixties and early seventies, Reg was the local representative of the RSPB for East Suffolk, and as such was privileged to enjoy the friendship of the late Bert Axell, then warden of Minsmere and creator of its 'scrape'. This was an era when there were more coypus than marsh harriers, more red-backed shrikes than bearded tits.

In 1973, Reg was one of the founder members of the Suffolk Ornithologists' Group, which has now grown into perhaps the most important bird-recording group in Suffolk. For the past thirty years he has also worked as a Government Wildlife Inspector specialising in birds of prey – a period when their numbers in the British Isles have dramatically increased. Although Reg had already cared for disabled wild owls and birds of prey for many years, being an Inspector gave him the opportunity to study these raptors from all parts of the world in great detail.

Reg's other main passion is his art. He paints not only the birds and animals he knows so well but, since the millennium, he has completed over two hundred portraits of the village people of Grundisburgh. His studio in that village is always open and welcoming to visitors.